Upgrade
Poems and Prose
by
Rex Moreton

First published by Root Creations, an imprint of Leaf Books
Ltd 2010

www.leafbooks.co.uk
Leaf Books Ltd.
GTi Suite,
Valleys Innovation Centre,
Navigation Park,
Abercynon,
CF45 4SN

Printed by Jem
www.jem.co.uk

ISBN-10: 1-905599-54-4
ISBN-13: 978-1-905599-54-7

Cover images: Rex Moreton

Contents

Upgrade

Very many years ago
She wrote with pen and ink
Smudges and blots in plenty
But it gave her time to think.

And then she had a fountain pen
A Parker fifty-one
She started writing poetry
And had a lot of fun.

Typewriter for her sixteenth
Her fingers flew over the keys
She thanked the lord for Tippex
And wrote short poems like these.

Sound the bugles, bang the drum
Computers have come to stay
She could write a poem in no time at all
If she knew what she wanted to say !

It's all so quick and easy
No time is left to think
The day her computer crashed
She poured herself a drink.

She took a swig, went out with the dog
And hired a boat on the lake,
She flew a kite. bought a bike
And called on her cousin Jake.

The repair man phoned and said 'It's done,
I expect you've really missed it.'
She said 'Not at all, I've been having a ball
And it's been lovely living without it!'

Is this Me?

Arthritis in the feet
A strain in the thigh
A pain in the ear
A twitch in the eye

Veins getting bulgy
Toenails growing in
Joints seizing up
Wrinkles in the skin

Old now and grotty
Not a pleasant sight
Looked in the mirror
Gave myself a fright

Devon Holiday

We gaze out of our expensive, luxury, holiday apartment's wall to wall windows. The plastic Venetian blinds adjusted to give the clearest possible view. The apartment looks across a quiet road to the sea. At nine o'clock on the first morning of our holiday a yellow van arrives and takes up its position across the road exactly opposite the apartment, it blocks our view of the sea. On the side of the van, in red lettering is written 'Locally made QUALITY DAIRY CREAM ICES'. Inside a young woman dons a hygienic white overall, opens the hatch and sits waiting patiently for customers. The morning is dull and grey, raining heavily, visibility poor. It is not possible to see the rocks at the end of the beach. By eleven thirty she hasn't sold a single ice cream. The ice cream lady puts an orange card in the window of the van with something written on it. This cannot be read from the apartment. She closes the serving hatch, takes off her white overall, climbs out of the van, locks the door, opens her umbrella and sets off at a brisk pace. As soon as she is out of sight a party of six holiday makers, muffled against the weather, gather round the serving hatch all wanting ice creams. They wait for several minutes then wander off along the promenade in the opposite direction to that taken by the ice cream lady.

When she returns to her van there is no sign of a customer. She lowers her umbrella and shakes it, unlocks the door of the van, climbs back in, dons her overall, removes the orange notice, sits down and opens her library book. She reads until seven o'clock in the evening with little interruption, then closes the hatch, removes her overall, sits behind the wheel, starts the engine and drives away.

It is the worst day of the season for ice cream sales, she hopes for a better day tomorrow but when she arrives at nine o'clock the next morning it is raining heavily and a strong breeze is blowing off the sea.

The Vegetarian

Close cropped hair, bags under his eyes
Always moaning and plenty of sighs
Lettuce sandwiches and dark brown bread.
And packets of nuts, remind me of Fred.

Fred's bed was lumpy and the pillow hard.
The dog was howling, out in the yard.
He couldn't sleep and got up for a pee
Looked at the clock, it was half past three

He took off his pyjamas and slowly dressed.
Went downstairs feeling very depressed.
His much-loved football, a bitter pill
Chelsea scoring twice and Arsenal nil.

Nothing in his life was worth a carrot.
Made much worse by the death of his parrot
Fred felt his life was getting worse.
He thought of flowers, he thought of a hearse.

He was only thirty, yet he felt ninety-one.
An ache in the head and a pain in the bum.
Into the garden and out through the gate.
Climbed the embankment, in suicidal state.

He made his way to the Arriva track.
Put his neck on the rail and lay on his back.
Fred thought of his holiday, booked in Spain .
He thought of his shares and their amazing gain.

He pictured Suzie, in her tight pink sweater.
And began to feel very much better.
He'd got it wrong! This was not his fate!
He tried to get up, but was just too late.

A Matter of Time

It was the view that clinched it
From the top of the cliff the endless sea
With cloudscapes, birds and passing ships.
She said 'Darling, we've got to buy it.'

But winter came with gales and storms.
A massive piece of the cliff went.
The following year was even worse
With the end of their garden taken.

They were warned 'The house will be next.'
There were no options, so they departed.
No money left, insurance none.
Miles away from the sea, they rented.

Twenty years later, they came again
Amazed at no further encroachment.
Their house still stood, neglected and sad.'
'It's only a matter of time.' he murmured.

Shopping List

When she writes her shopping list
It's like a poet's rhyme
Sausages and onions
And a little sprig of thyme.

A bottle of Spanish sherry
Two tins of custard
Hartley's strawberry jam
A jar of Coleman's mustard

When she's busy writing it
She's as quiet as a mouse
When we reach the superstore
She's left it in the house.

Outlook

Twelve year old Julie called on her widowed grandpa on the way home from school.

He made a pot of tea and opened a new packet of chocolate biscuits, they sat at the kitchen table and he said, 'Many years ago, Julie, we sent letters to each other. We used paper and wrote by hand using a thing called a 'pen'

Our new pens had ball points and never needed filling, a few people still used 'fountain pens' which had nibs and periodically needed to be refilled with ink, I remember The favourite colour was blue black but other colours were available, aunt May favoured purple… we all know what she was like!

When completed we sealed the letter in an envelope on which the recipient's name and address was written. A postage stamp of the appropriate value attached to the top right hand corner for first or second class and then dropped into a bright red pillar box where – you won't believe this Julie – it was collected and delivered by hand. If a reply was needed it could take three or four days before you received it!

It came to be known as 'snail mail' you can see why!

We were taught 'hand-writing' at school, not like today Julie, where they teach you how to tap out messages at high speed on a keypad without even looking at it. What you write can be seen on a screen, corrections and alterations made in seconds and a clever device will make sure your spelling is correct.

Nowadays an e-mail can be sent to the recipient and a reply received in minutes, not like in my day!

Of course these devices can print a hard copy or we can simply store a lifetime's work which will be accessible forever.

We don't even need to type out a message; we can see each other on the screen and share conversations anywhere in the world.

Things have come so far and are so brilliant it's a shame about the disaster of global warming and the spread of pollution and disease, forty per cent of the planet is already uninhabitable. The rain forests are no more, the ice caps are melting faster than ever and the population explosion means we can't grow sufficient crops to feed everyone… millions are starving.

We have only ourselves to blame, selfishness and greed at the root of the problem.

According to the papers our world has about twenty years to go, maximum, then it will all be finished.

Our only hope is the new planet they've discovered and named 'Sanctum' but it's on the outer edge of our solar system and so far we have no means of reaching it.

I know they're colonising the moon as a staging post but only anticipate sending the brightest under thirties up there, which rules me out. Only one in fifty thousand will be selected.

Seven nations are be working together on the project but all they seem to do is argue! Then there's this new drug, meant to extend human life to three hundred years… sounds horrible to me! They think it will be needed for the trip to Sanctum, and so far they don't even have a craft which could complete a voyage of this magnitude!

I honestly think it would be better to finish it now, it's going to be absolutely ghastly.'

He opened a drawer in the kitchen table and took out his illegal world war two Webley and Scott revolver. Before Julie could move he muttered, 'It's for the best.' And shot the schoolgirl in the head before turning the gun on himself.

Little Willie and the Crocodile

Our big fat scout leader
Was trying not to smile
He said 'Naughty little Willie
Has been eaten by a crocodile.'

Willie down by the river
Was catching lots of fish
When out jumped a crocodile
And swallowed the tasty dish.

Inside the crocodile
It was hot and dark and smelly
Willie with his 'Boy scout' knife
Cut a hole in the crocodile's belly.

Out popped little Willie
From the hole in the crocodile's side
Willie still was fighting fit
It was the crocodile that died.

Beachy Head

He parked his eleven year old car on the short grass. The wind sighing, drizzling rain, a heavy grey sky... perfectly matching his mood.

Thirty years old next week and still living with his parents... he knew he was a failure.

He slipped a CD into the player and sat listening to a mournful Leonard Cohen track. He remembered a music critic calling it 'Music to commit suicide to.'

He listened until the track ended and leaving the key in the ignition and the music still playing made his way to the fence. He found a vandal made gap and squeezed through it.

He walked slowly to the cliff edge and sat with his legs dangling.

He observed the lighthouse 500 ft below, its bright colours muted by the gloom of the day.

As he began to push himself over the edge his mobile phone rang. He took it from his jacket pocket, switched it off and with as much force as his seated position allowed, hurled it into space.

He spotted a uniformed figure approaching, the man waved to him in greeting, he waved back and then launched himself over the edge.

He found the sense of falling wonderfully exhilarating, but short lived.

He struck the cliff face with great force. Jagged unbearable pain.

The second time he hit the side he lost consciousness.

By the time he crashed onto the rocks at the foot of the cliff he was already dead.

In his car the music was still playing.

I Love You

I love you in the daytime
I love you when it's night
I love you in your curlers
When you look a perfect fright.

I love you when you're naked
I love you fully clad
I love you when you're good
But more so when you're bad.

I love you in the winter
The summer and the fall
In spring when sap is rising
I love you most of all.

I love to see you cooking
With flour upon your nose
And peeping in the oven
To make sure your sponges rose.

I love you in the sunshine
And in the pouring rain
I remember thunder and lightning
When my love was like a pain.

I loved you when you were twenty
I loved you at fifty-five
And now although we've past our best
The love is still alive.

I love you in the mountains
I love you in the dales
But most of all I love you
When you come home again to Wales.

Astronaut

This new craft is infinitely faster than anything we have previously built; it will orbit the earth in only fifteen minutes. It has been said that at this speed every circuit of the earth will make the occupant a week younger, but of course this is complete nonsense.

The cabin is pressurised, temperature controlled and extremely comfortable, no special clothes need to be worn.

The newly developed pills contain all the nutrients needed for the two month period you will be in orbit. You will have no sensation of speed, the acceleration is gentle.

They shook hands with him, closed the hatch and carried out the launch.

As the weeks passed he realised he was becoming smaller, his hands were like the hands of a schoolboy, his feet slipped out of his shoes and the tracksuit became ridiculously loose. His chin was smooth, his hair blonde and curly.

As the days passed he knew less and less.

When they brought the craft in and opened the hatch he was a small sticky patch.

Three Clerihews

Andrew Motion
Struck by a notion
Having nothing else to do
Wrote a clerihew

Tim Rice
Was awfully nice
When asked for his autograph
He wrote a paragraph

Charles Phillip Arthur George Prince of Wales
Bought a suit in the winter sales
His mother said 'Charles, you do look a fright
Don't wear it in daylight, only at night.

(Named after Edmund Clerihew Bentley who invented the form)
Four lines, famous person in first line. A&B rhyme and C&D rhyme

Three More

Albert Einstein Doing His Sums
Used all his fingers and both of his thumbs
When calculators came
It was not the same.

He who was God
Said 'What a sod
There's sunshine in Devon
And I'm stuck here in heaven.'

Isaac Newton Struck by an Apple
With laws of gravity began to grapple
He polished the fruit and took a bite
Thoughts of gravity soon took flight.

The Saturday Dig

Rain or shine, hot or cold; it was the same thing every Saturday morning. Collect the big spade from the shed. Go down to the tiny brick building at the bottom of the garden and open the shabby, rickety door. To see inside the dark interior a wooden seat with a round hole cut in the middle, the edges chamfered to make it comfortable to sit on. Lift the hinged wooden seat, nice and clean, regularly scrubbed by my mother and carefully remove the heavy bucket from underneath. Leave the seat up to be sure no one will mistakenly use the lav while the bucket is absent. Carry it into the garden being careful not to splash any of the contents over the side. Pick up the spade; dig a suitable size hole and trying not to breathe too deeply gently pour the contents of the bucket into it. Shovel earth back into the hole being even more careful to avoid splashing.

A mental record of recent deposits was useful, but to begin with a mental record was unfortunately something I didn't have. So on one or two occasions when I placed my foot on the spade and firmly drove it into the ground it came up with a soggy, sludgy smelly load on it.

My mum said this work was 'A man's job' at twelve years old I was the only male in the cottage so it was obvious I should be the one to do it.

The village gardeners grew rows of runner beans with prolific yields and their root vegetables were spectacular... I knew their secret!

After Mum and Dad were divorced before the war, Mum took my sister and me to live at Clacton-on-sea in Essex to be near her sister. Shortly after the war started we children were evacuated to Gloucestershire, labels tied on us and gas masks in cardboard boxes hung round our necks. Mum had arranged for our furniture to be taken into storage and soon followed us down. She found this cottage, had our furniture moved down and then retrieved us from our foster parents so we could be

19

together again.

I missed the amenities we had enjoyed in a large seaside town, particularly the indoor flushing toilet, the bathroom and the electricity. I suppose we were poor but Mum drove a Post Office van to supplement the payments received from Dad and we were happy enough in our little cottage.

One Saturday, after the digging and filling in was completed I replaced the bucket, shut the door and sat on the seat. I read for the hundredth time the verse on the back of the door, written I supposed, by some previous occupant who had been kept waiting outside. I know Mum thought it offensive but I thought it was jolly good.

And then, a couple of weeks later she said 'I've got a job for you' and produced a paint brush and a can of creosote, 'When you've done the bucket you can paint the lavatory door, you can have an extra sixpence with your pocket money.'

'Just the outside?'

'No both sides, and make sure you do a good job.'

I did a thorough job and the verse disappeared forever.

But I can still remember it.

'We don't come here
To sit and ponder
But to shit and piss
And fart like thunder.'

Sluggard

He opened bleary eyes
And looked at the clock
Four minutes after eight!

The alarm had sounded at seven.
With outstretched arm
And the press of a finger
He'd stopped the racket.

Eyes closed, he'd drifted back to sleep.
Now at four minutes after eight
He moved.
Slid his legs from the cosy bed
Into the chill of the room.

He stood, ran fingers through his hair.
Made his way to the window
Drew back the heavy curtains.
Looked at the stormy sky
The heavy pouring rain and
Trees buffeted by the gale.

After a few seconds he closed the curtains,
Murmured 'Bloody awful weather.'
Crossed the room and climbed back
Into the warm and welcoming bed.

Feeling guilty he closed his eyes.
Soon overcame any trace of guilt
After a few more minutes
He was deeply, snoringly, asleep.

Apple Cart

Farmer Phipps said gruffly 'You want to come into town with me boy?'

He always called him boy.

The boy was an evacuee, he lived in Farmer Phipps' ancient stone farmhouse. The farmer was a widower but his grown daughter looked after both of them. The boy was scared of Farmer Phipps; all the village boys were scared of him.

But a trip to town by horse and cart would be a rare treat so he said, 'Yes please sir.' 'Go round and wait by the barn door then, I'll fetch the cart; the apples are in sacks ready to be loaded.' The boy waited in the open doorway breathing in the mouth-watering smell of the orchard apples, which were the reason for the trip. Farmer Phipps soon came round with the huge horse pulling a two wheel cart. He set to work and loaded the apples; the sacks were too heavy to be lifted by a twelve year old boy so he kept out of the way and watched the farmer working.

When all the sacks were in the cart, he said, 'Better climb in if you're coming boy.' The boy clambered in, the farmer flicked the reins, made a clicking noise with his tongue and they were off on the three-mile journey to town. They jolted their way through narrow country lanes, the sun shining brightly and the hedges full of birds.

The boy kept glancing at the open sacks of rosy apples and remembered the delicious Coxes Orange Pippins Mrs Allen had given him at his previous foster home.

These looked even better, his mouth watered.

As they jogged along the huge horse kept noisily breaking wind, Farmer Phipps took no notice but the boy was acutely embarrassed. In spite of his embarrassment he found it hilariously funny and desperately wanted to laugh, it was a struggle to smother his giggles.

The boy kept looking at the apples; Farmer Phipps had his eye on the road ahead so he took his chance and helped himself to a nice red one out of the nearest sack and hid it behind his back. He felt a certain amount of guilt, but more a sense of

22

achievement. He waited for a few minutes and then, feeling it was reasonably safe to do so, took a great bite out of it. It was horrible, sourer than you would think possible, especially when it looked so tempting, his teeth stood on edge. He leaned over the back of the cart, spat it out and threw the rest of the apple after it. Who on earth would be stupid enough to buy apples that tasted like this?

He said, 'Excuse me sir,' Farmer Phipps looked round and nodded, so he said 'Who are the apples for?' He just looked at the boy and for a few moments the boy thought he wasn't going to speak but then he said, 'Arthur Clissold from the Fountain Inn at Bisley, he's coming down in his van to pick them up.'

'What's he going to do with them sir?'

'He's got a press and he's going to make them into cider to sell in his pub... now be quiet and stop pestering me boy.'

'Sorry sir.' he said, and shut up but he thought it's going to be awful cider unless Mr Clissold puts a lot of sugar in it.

Eventually they turned into the yard of the Red Lion and Farmer Phipps said, 'Jump out boy.' And climbed out after him. He put the nosebag on the horse and looking round the yard said 'Can't see his van, don't think he's here yet, come and hold the horse for me while I go and have a look in the bar for him.'

He must have seen the look of terror on the boy's face, he said 'No need to worry boy, Samson's as good as gold, gentle as a lamb he's not going to give you any trouble.' The boy gingerly approached the front end of the horse and Farmer Phipps showed him where to hold the bridle and went off to look for Mr Clissold.

Samson showed no inclination to move and after a few minutes the boy's terror subsided. After a few more minutes he began to feel proud of being in charge of such a huge beast and hoped some of his school friends might pass and see him, but none did. Then Samson stamped one of his massive front feet and with this ground shaking event the boy's terror returned.

By now, Samson was munching placidly on the contents of his nosebag and the boy became bored, he began to think it would be jolly good if he could climb up and sit on the horses back. He looked for a way to do it but realised it would mean letting go of the bridle and then Samson might decide to walk. He tried to think of other diversions but before he could do anything stupid a small grey van arrived and a fat man with a big moustache got out. He walked over and asked, 'Are you with Mr Phipps, lad and are those apples for me?' The boy said 'Yes sir, they are if you're Mr Clissold from the Fountain… he's gone into the pub to look for you.' He hoped he wouldn't taste an apple to see if they were all right. 'I'll pop in and look for him.' he said. But at that moment Farmer Phipps came out of the pub, the two men shook hands and the boy was relieved of his horse minding duty. Farmer Phipps led Samson over to the van and tethered him to it; the two men quickly loaded the sacks into the back of the van and locked the doors.

Farmer Phipps felt in his pocket, took out some change and gave the boy tuppence. 'Thank you very much sir.' he said. 'You can go up the street and buy yourself some sweets, we're going to have a drink in the bar, don't be too long though, you can wait for me in the cart if I'm not here.'

The boy went to the top of the street but didn't buy sweets, Farmer Phipps had forgotten to give him any coupons so he bought a bag of deliciously, sweet apples instead.

Supermarket Incident

Outside Tesco's the ambulance stood ready
They helped her out, she was very unsteady.
She was closely followed by her heaped up trolley
An assistant ran out, 'Don't forget your brolly.'

A customer remarked, 'Ambulance service is swell
They'll take her home now, her shopping as well.'
I said to the medic 'Is she seriously ill?'
He said 'She fainted when they gave her the bill.'

Her husband in the garden pulling up weeds
He'd had no coffee, she was neglecting his needs!
It gave him a turn, seeing the ambulance arrive
When the driver reached him, he was no longer alive.

Twenty names

Pearl Fisher
Laura Norder
Tom Boyes
Sonia Foot
Norman Castle
Lily White
Pearl E Gates
Jack Hammer
Ben Dover
Olive Groves
Haydn Secombe
Emma Royds
Albert Ross
Carol Singer
Percy Vere
Jo King
Albert Hall
Nesta Robins
Penny Farthing
Robin Banks

Girl in the Forest

The girl walked through the forest as she did every Thursday, taking vital provisions to her disabled but much loved granny. The strong breeze whistling through the trees blew her new red dress against her legs. The Tesco 'Bag for life' she carried contained the usual two bottles of Gordon's Gin and half a dozen bottles of tonic water. Enough to last her gran until next Thursday.

She reached the cottage and let herself in. The room was dim, curtains drawn and the bedside lamp switched off, She could make out the figure in the bed, but in the gloom didn't realize it was a wolf in granny's clothing.

She went over to the bed and said, 'I've brought the booze gran.' She bent down to kiss the old lady and became aware of an unusual smell. The next second the wolf bit her head off.

She dropped the 'Bag for life' and one of the bottles of gin broke, all the bottles of tonic water survived.

A burly wood-cutter burst in, drew back the curtains, saw the headless girl and the wolf in granny's bed. With one mighty blow of his axe he cut off the wolf's head.

He was the only one who lived happily ever after.

Word Game

'I know a new game.'
'Shall we play it?'
'OK, think of a word.'
'Any word I like?'
'Whatever comes to mind.'
'Sex.'
'Except that one.'
'Er… money.'
'Pick another.'
'Booze.'
'Look, if all you can think of
is sex, money and booze
we'd better play something else.'

Dentist

Sitting in the dentist's chair
In a fully reclined position
A spotlight shining on my face
Dazzling my eyes, I shut them.

Mouth wide open,
Padding round the gums,
Something hooked over lower teeth
Disgusting sucking sounds.

While probing molars he asks
'How are you today?'
I try to reply and manage to say
'Inge yust hine, hanks herry hutch.'

Sonnet

Shall I compare thee to a London bus?
Thou art so big and plump and rosy.
Winds in thy stomach may cause a fuss
But I bury my nose in a perfumed posy.
Sometimes in heat thy perspiration shines
And often is thy stretched complexion red.
But thou thy coal black hair defines
Unkempt and tumbling, newly from the bed
But thy ephemeral voluptuousness may fade
And what thou are shall never more be seen.
We both too soon will move into the shade
And what we were may not have ever been.
      So long as men can breathe, or eyes can see,
      So long lives this, and this gives life to thee.

The Last two lines are from William Shakespeare's Sonnet 18

Visit to the Park

Ruth Jackson can't get back to sleep; she's been awakened by her recurring nightmare, thankfully, not as frequent now as it had once been.

In this dream, she re-lives the horror of the car crash, which, five years ago, killed her much-loved husband and deprived her of eighty per cent of the use of her legs.

Although it's much too early to get up she decides she will anyway and climbs stiffly out of bed. She showers, dresses, eats some bran flakes, enjoys a cup of coffee, puts on her make-up, hangs a camera round her neck and with the aid of a sturdy walking stick makes her way to the mobility scooter in the garage. The little red scooter has transformed her life, Ruth loves it. Bright and shiny with four fat white rubber tyres, which fortunately never need to be pumped up. It looks smart, business like and is great fun to drive. Powered by a big rechargeable battery it can travel at eight miles an hour, faster than most folks walk!

The wrought iron park gates bearing the city's colourful coat of arms, are not only handsome, but standing open.

Ruth drives through, the trees in the park are huge, ancient and magnificent, they are the reason for bringing her camera. She glides through the park and stops the scooter beside her favourite seat.

She struggles off the scooter and eases herself onto the bench.

The sun is well up now and provides perfect lighting for the trees. She raises the camera to her eye, composes a picture, focuses and presses the button to capture the image.

A grey squirrel arrives; she zooms the lens to the telephoto setting and takes a few shots. She continues to sit on the bench, not taking photographs, simply enjoying the solitude and the antics of the squirrel.

She notices someone in the distance, walking down the path in her direction. She tries to look at the figure without appearing to stare. As the man gets closer, he seems strange to her, a dropout she decides and feels rather anxious.

He's wearing a long, old-fashioned fawn raincoat, which comes well below his knees, his legs are bare and his feet in the worn sandals are without socks. Ruth thinks 'Must have escaped from somewhere.' and hopes he won't want to sit on her bench. She feels a little ashamed of her thoughts.

When the man reaches the bench, he says politely, in a pleasant voice 'May I share your seat with you for a few minutes?'

Surprisingly, she feels no sense of threat and says 'Please do.'

He settles beside Ruth and they both sit watching the squirrel; he turns to Ruth and says 'One of God's little creatures, very entertaining, aren't they?' Ruth, remembers reading somewhere that grey squirrels are vermin and says 'Yes, I suppose they are.' She has no wish to be drawn into conversation with this strange man.

The squirrel scampers over to them hoping for food. It jumps onto the man's lap and sits on his knee. 'Well he's certainly got a way with animals' thinks Ruth. The stranger strokes the squirrel's head with his finger. After a few minutes, the squirrel jumps back down to the ground, climbs one of the trees and soon disappears from sight.

The man looks at Ruth with sad blue eyes, smiles and asks 'Do you live around here?'

Always polite she says 'Yes, just up the road, Park Crescent , what about you?'

The man lifts his chin and says 'Up there.'

'Not giving much away' thinks Ruth.

'This is my second coming' the man says 'but nobody has taken any notice of me.'

Ruth decides she was right... he's a nutter for sure.' And

fervently hopes he'll leave soon.

'It's much worse now than it was the last time I was here' he says.

'Things are in a mess' she agrees 'no doubt about that.'

Ruth studies her unwelcome companion and thinks 'At least he looks clean and he doesn't smell, he has a healthy complexion and his beard is well cared for.' After a few more minutes and without further conversation he gets to his feet. 'I shall go now and leave you in peace.'

He holds out his hand and as Ruth shakes it, says 'May I ask please, what is your name?'

' Jackson ' she says politely 'Ruth Jackson, and yours?'

He lays his other hand on her arm and says 'Jesus... Jesus of Nazareth .'

And disappears.

Ruth can't believe it, one second here, large as life and the next second gone!' She can feel a prickling sensation in the hair on the back of her head.

She prepares to struggle up off the bench and onto the scooter but stands as easily as though she was eighteen again. She places the walking stick in its holder and walks briskly up the path for twenty or thirty yards, there is no pain and no fear of loosing her balance.

In her uplifted state, she actually runs back to the scooter. She hasn't been able to run for five years!

Ruth rides her scooter home, puts it away in the garage and walks down to the. Church, experiencing once more the joy of walking. She goes inside and kneels in one of the pews, she is struck by the beauty of the interior and the sense of peace. She offers up a heartfelt prayer which includes a heartfelt 'Thank-you'

Who is She ?

She is her husband's wife
She is her mother's daughter
She is her daughter's mother
She is her brother's sister
She is her grandchild's granny
She is her pupil's teacher
She is her garden's gardener
She is her patient's nurse
She is her doctor's patient
She is her friend's friend
She is her enemy's enemy
She is her mirror's reflection
She is her cake's baker
She is her essay's writer
She is her lover's lover
She is her horse's rider
She is her dog's walker
She is her car's driver
She is her birthday's thirty-fourth
She is her choir's top note
She is her W.I,s' secretary
She is the one who says 'yes'
   When everyone else is saying 'No'
She is much more than all of this
She is the giver of life.

En Suite

He opened the door and stepped into the small, dark, windowless, room.

He grasped the porcelain egg shaped fitting on the end of a cord and pulled it down A loud click, the light came on and a fan in the ceiling began to spin.

Slowly at first but soon gaining speed.

He found the noise, amplified by the hard, tiled, walls unbelievably irritating.

He sat waiting patiently, bored, miserable and without result.

He wished he'd brought a newspaper with him to read.

He sat for ten more minutes then gave up the struggle.

Conference starting in twenty minutes.

He pressed the flush button, more from habit than necessity.

When he came out, he was even more depressed than when he went in.No help for it, he'd have to more pills.

Blackbirds

No blackbirds in our garden
No blackbirds in the sky
Four and twenty of them
Baked in a dainty pie.

When the pie was opened
The birds began to sing
When it comes to nursery rhymes
You can't believe a thing.

Measurements

At seven-fifteen the alarm clock woke Ernie Foot, fifty years old, five feet ten inches tall, forty two inch chest, thirty eight inch waist, twenty eight inch inside leg, shoe size ten and a half.

In nineteen and a half minutes he was washed and on his way down the twelve stair treads to his eleven by nine kitchen. He ate his usual breakfast. Two boiled eggs, three pieces of toast, one cup of coffee with two spoonfuls of sugar. Breakfast had taken twenty-nine minutes.

The washing-up took another seven minutes; he went out of the back door and down three steps to the garden. He opened the boot of his 1986 Ford Cortina in readiness and made his way to the bottom of his one eighth acre garden. He entered his twenty feet by eight feet greenhouse where he cut through the three inch stalk of his massive marrow, four feet long, five feet two inches girth and sixty-seven pounds in weight. He struggled up the garden with it and safely loaded it into the car. He made a three point turn and drove the four and a half miles to the showground at an average speed of thirty-one miles an hour, arriving at eight-seventeen.

He carried his marrow into the sixty foot marquee and placed it in the allotted place on the eight feet by three feet trestle table. During the morning three judges did their work and Ernie's marrow won first prize. He was presented with a silver cup nine inches high and eight point four troy ounces in weight. His for twelve months.

He went to The Six Bells and drank four pints of bitter; on his way out he tripped and fell onto the bag containing the cup. His fall made two dents in it.

A breath of fresh air

They were no longer young, he'd been married twice
She was ahead of him, she'd been married thrice.
They were enjoying the cruise and loved being at sea
And happily honeymooning, there was plenty to see.

He smiled as he said 'What could be finer
Than us making love on this grand ocean liner?'
They enjoyed Venus' sports on the large comfy bed
And lay close together as they sailed through the Med.

They loved it in the evening, their sex was like heaven.
She got out her book 'Shall we try number seven?'
He said, 'You're a star and it isn't too late,
If you're sure you feel up to it, we could try number eight.'

When he climbed off the bed and threw on his gown
She asked 'Where are you going?' He noticed her frown.
He stood before the mirror and straightened his hair
'I'm going on deck' he said, 'For a breath of fresh air.'

Saturday Morning

Timothy opened his eyes and became aware of daylight filtering through a gap in the thick velvet bedroom curtains. Elaine was not in bed beside him. He rolled over and looked at the alarm clock with annoyance; he should have been out of bed an hour ago. His annoyance increased, why hadn't she roused him?

Of course! It's Saturday; no rush then.

He slid out of bed, went down to the kitchen, made himself a pot of tea, poured a cup and sat at the table drinking it, the kitchen floor cool to his bare feet.

He put his cup and saucer in the dish-washer, wandered back upstairs, opened the bathroom door without knocking and went in.

Elaine, fresh from her bath, pink and voluptuous, standing on the bathroom scales, smiling at him invitingly. He moved closer, put his hands on her hips, gave her a lingering kiss and said 'you look extremely pleased with yourself this morning darling!'

He began to slowly move his hands.

'Don't be naughty Timothy!' she said without conviction; I've every right - stop it you devil - to feel pleased with myself, it's a red letter day for me.

Since I started the course I've lost a stone!'

Some People

Some are short and some are long
Some smell sweet while others pong.
Some are week and some are strong
Some are athletes and win a gong.

Some are filthy some are clean
Some are holy, some obscene.
Some are happy, some are sad
Some are good but most are bad.

Some are bright and some are slow
If asked the time, they wouldn't know.
Some in sunshine, some in rain
Some in comfort and some in pain.

Some are fat, some are thin
Others are simply bones and skin.
Some are colourful, some are drab
Like rainbow fish compared to crab.
Some like nature and hugging trees
Having an affinity with birds and bees.
Some like swimming, some like to hike
Others like to pedal for miles on a bike.

Some get high and some do not
Some like alcohol some prefer pot.
Some like sex and can be outrageous
They like to do it if it's not contagious.

Some are sick and some are healthy
Some are poor and some are wealthy.
Some wrote poems, some wrote prose
William Shakespeare was the best of those.

The Puppy

Mum let me have a puppy, I've called him Fred
She says I must keep him in the garden shed.
'Cause he poo'd in the kitchen and on the rug in the hall
And when it comes to peeing, he'll go anywhere at all.

He's grown very big, an Alsatian cross
I'm afraid it's not me, it's him who's boss.
We've just had a visit from glamorous aunty Meg
That naughty wicked dog bit her shapely leg.

He killed next-door's cat, bit off its head
Said the next door lady 'It's that damn dog Fred.'
When he sees the postman he's full of hate
Won't let the poor man in through the gate.

When he bit my dad, he said, 'I've had enough
I'll take him to the vet, let him to do his stuff.
So Fred's gone up to big dog heaven
Too much of a problem for a boy of seven.

Sailor

The day that I was seventeen
I sailed away to sea
I had a girl in every port
And sometimes two or three

When I was twenty-one years old
I met sweet Sarah-Jane
We married in September
And I never sailed again

The Bus Driver and the Lottery

I want to be rich, I want to act dirty
And go out with girls who are pretty and flirty.
I want to own Bentleys and Astons and Rolls
And go out for rides with sexy blonde molls.
Drink buckets of champagne and glasses of brandy
Eat caviar and oysters until I feel randy.
I want to have bank accounts stuffed full of money
And villas in places where the weather is sunny.
I want a digital camera, a Nikon would be nice
And a selection of lenses regardless of price.
I want a white yacht, at least ninety feet long
I want to be honoured and given a gong.
I want to wear top hats, have strings of horses
And swagger about at the poshest racecourses.
Executive jets? Yes I think I'll have two
With an elegant hostess and subservient crew.
I want a physician to look after my health
And financial advisers to safeguard my wealth.
I must get on my bike and pedal to work
The lads at the depot all think I'm a berk.

Harry and the Blunderbuss

The sun shining, the sky blue, birds singing. Harry at peace with the world, out on the prowl. He usually called at larger properties particularly those that looked run down as there was more chance of finding worthwhile antiques. But this pretty cottage with an inviting notice propped on the gate announcing 'VEG FOR SALE' was too good to miss.

He strolled down the garden path, observing rows of vegetables, neat, orderly and weed free. The wooden porch, painted bright blue but softened by a prolific climbing rose, a mass of blooms this sunny morning.

In answer to his knock, the door was opened by a small grey haired man. Harry noted the bright blue eyes, matching the paintwork of the porch, his manner cheerful and as neat in appearance as his garden.

Harry's attention was immediately drawn to the blunderbuss hanging on the wall just inside the door. The brass barrel dull, the gun dusty and seemingly neglected but seeming to be in good order, he hoped to be able to buy it before leaving. Harry gave him his business card and introduced himself, the occupant said his name was Lewis. They shook hands.

'Antiques is it?'

'Yes, but I'd like some vegetables' so they went into the garden. Harry bought potatoes, leeks, a large cauliflower and some onions, at the same time they enjoyed animated and interesting conversation.

'What about a few strawberries.'

'I didn't spot any, but I'd like some.'

'They're round the back, how many?'

'Enough for three, please.'

They went behind the cottage, another piece of garden, smaller but just as neat and mostly given over to flowers, a riot of colour. They went to the strawberry patch and Lewis handed

Harry a punnet, pick what you'd like sir.'

Harry said, 'Harry.'

Lewis grinned and said, 'Pick what you'd like Harry.'

Harry said, 'I'd like a nice bunch of flowers for my wife, I'll let you choose them.' When a colourful bunch had been selected he said, 'What do I owe you?'

The gardener named a price which to Harry seemed much too little.

'Are you sure that's enough?'

'Quite enough Harry thank you, I enjoy the garden and growing things. Being retired there's plenty of time. But the big problem is the slugs. I do hate slugs, don't know where they all come from, I collected fifty-two yesterday evening... they come out at dusk, that's the best time to catch the blighters.'

Harry removed a bunch of notes from his back pocket and as was his habit, made sure they were seen by Lewis as he peeled off a ten pound note.

'Have to go into the house for some change.' This suited Harry well. He waited in the porch and when Lewis returned with his change said, 'What about that gun, would you think of selling it, I collect old guns?'

'Wouldn't mind, used to like it but now it's just one more thing needing to be dusted, time I did it again by the look of it!'

He took it down from the wall and handed it to Harry. As Harry took it, it went off. There was a deafening explosion, a hole appeared in the porch roof and the climbing rose collapsed in an untidy heap.

'Crikey! Said Lewis in a shocked voice, 'Had it all these years and never knew it was loaded. Now at least we know it's in working order!'

Harry offered fifty pounds and apologised for the hole in the porch roof.

'Not your fault Harry, I can easily patch it, give it a fresh coat of paint and retrain the poor old rose. Fifty pounds is OK.

You take the gun, I'll bring these bags to the car for you. I hope you'll come again for some more veg now you've found me; runner beans should be starting next week, best when they're young.' They shook hands and Harry drove away having made a new friend.

It was not until he'd been driving for five minutes that he began to shake. Harry's vivid imagination took over. Supposing the gun had been pointing at Lewis when it went off, it would have blown his head to pieces, or lower down it would still have killed him. Think of the hole in the porch roof! My God, a knocker at the door and the occupant shot dead... murder! He could have been done for murder, years in jail. He tried not to think about it, the harder he tried the worse it was. He drove back to Mulberry House, left everything in the car, went into the house, drank a glass of whisky, went upstairs, took off his shoes and climbed into bed.

When Maria returned from her shopping trip she saw the Volvo but no sign of Harry. The last place she looked was their bedroom and there he was, sound asleep in bed with all his clothes on and smelling strongly of whisky. She thought, he'd better tell me what's going on. She took hold of his shoulder and shook him, he woke with a start.

'What on earth's going on Harry, why are you in bed with all your clothes on and drinking whisky in the middle of the day?'

'I nearly shot a man with a blunderbuss, luckily it missed him. Judging by the damage to his porch it would definitely finished him off. It would be seen as murder... a knocker at the door, I'd sure to have been banged up for years... what a bloody disaster! I'm going to stay here in bed out of harm's way.'

'Don't be such a baby, you haven't killed anyone, even if you had it would most likely be seen as a tragic accident.

'This blunderbuss – did you buy it?'

'I did, it's still in the car, and some freshly picked veg and strawberries and a nice bunch of flowers for you love'

46

'You'd better get up, we'll unload the car, I'll put the flowers in water and then make us a pot of tea, you'll soon feel better.'

While Maria made the tea Harry worked on the gun, cleaning the dust and accumulated dirt off it, oiling it and polishing it until it glowed, the brass barrel looked particularly fine. By the time he'd finished he suggested to Maria she should make another pot of tea and they ate the strawberries leaving enough for Lucy when she came in from school.

'It looks so good Harry, will you sell it to Patrick?'

'I think I will, he'd love it and I couldn't stand people messing about with it if I took it to the antique centre. Patrick will pay a good price for it, keep it for himself I expect. When I've recovered from the shock I'll run it over to him… make his day.'

Red Wine

With a big beefy spread
I always drink red
If it's fish or it's light
Well then I drink white

I'm an expert on booze
So I can help you to choose
The best sort of liqueur
To move things on quicker

If you just want good cheer
Stick to tankards of beer
If you want girls more frisky
Then give them Scotch whisky

A glassful of rum
Puts a glow in the tum
A few measures of brandy
Will make everyone randy.

If you want 'rumpy pumpy'
You'll never beat scrumpy.
But for an evening of sin
Serve them plenty of gin.

I've followed this advice
And been married twice
It's not what I'd choose
It was caused by the booze.

Haunted House

He felt very alone in the dark empty house
Nothing else lived here, not even a mouse.
From down in the cellar a rattle of chain
He stood stock-still and heard it again.

His torch began to flicker and then went out
Scared out of his wits he wanted to shout.
Something putrid brushed over his cheek
His legs began trembling, he felt dreadfully weak.

In his face he felt a foul icy breath
He knew what it was; the strong smell of death.
He collapsed to the floor in an untidy heap
Closed both of his eyes, he was going to sleep.

He could no longer move, his body grew cold
Found two days later, the police were soon told.
The chief of police said 'It seems rather strange
This has happened before, down at the Grange.'

He said to his sergeant 'Find out what you can
Don't spend too much time on this scruffy old man.'
The post mortem showed no murder or crime
Natural causes were blamed, which saved the police time.

Naughty Boy

Behind my back you pull faces and sneer
You really deserved that clip round the ear?
You kicked Uncle Tom and you bit Aunty Jane
For bad behaviour, you were whacked with the cane.

I just heard you call me an ugly old trout
As soon as I catch you, I'll give you a clout
You're very unruly, you answered me back
So I picked up the shovel and gave you a whack.

I *meant* that to hurt, so you'd best stop that row
Or you'll soon find out I'm a hardhearted cow.
If you keep up this howling, you won't make old bones
I swear this is true or my name isn't Jones.

You being so naughty is driving me mad
So when he comes home I shall speak to your dad.
A note from your teacher says 'disruptive in class'
You'd better bend over for six on the arse.

An unwelcome visit to the home of the Jones
Drew from his mother hard-done-by groans.
Miss Clegg from the welfare wrote in her pad
'The way his mum treats him, no wonder he's bad.'

Rosemary's New Dress

Out from the changing room,
Swinging her hips
Tom said, 'It's lovely.'
He was licking his lips
'We've seen half a dozen,
This one is nice.'
'She said 'Shall we take it?'
He said, 'Look at the price!'

… *'But you're worth it.'*

Snapshot

That's not me
Yes it is
It can't be me
Well it is
I'm not that fat
Yes you are
It's the angle of the camera
No it's not
It must be the lens
Don't be daft
It's just not me
How tall are you?
Five foot four
What do you weigh?
Fifteen stone
There you are then!

Upstairs Window

The Internet is wonderful. I have always enjoyed buying things and now, from the comfort of my home, with a few clicks of the mouse, I have access to just about anything I could ever need or desire. I buy clothes, books and CD's and sometimes larger items from stores I can no longer manage to visit.

My exercise bike came in a large, cardboard crate. I unpacked it and when my son called in for coffee he carried all the pieces upstairs and assembled it for me in the spare room.

Believe me, pedalling for fifteen minutes without moving off the spot is tedious and after a week I was ready to give up but my daughter pointed out that using the exercise bike was not just beneficial for the legs, the reason I'd bought it, but good for the heart and several other parts of the body as well. Together we moved the exercise bike closer to the window. From here I could look up the road and observe any interesting activity. I agreed to persevere.

There was some excitement at the start of the second week. Our house is on a corner, I can look up the main road or straight across the Crescent at the big Victorian house opposite. It is three storeys high and built of stone. A massive tree stands in the garden. The general appearance is dark and forbidding. The curtains are always drawn and nobody is seen going in or out.

My pedal rate slowed as several police cars and a van turned into the Crescent

Soon the garden opposite was full of uniformed police and people in white overalls. They smashed their way in through the front door and were soon carrying out large cannabis plants in pots. More plants were thrown down from an upstairs window.

Finally they led out a small, elderly Vietnamese man. In the local paper he was quoted as saying 'The bosses sent me down from London to do gardening.'

Ten year old Sophie said 'Grandpa why do the policemen take the cannabis plants away?' I said 'Some people like to put the cannabis in cigarettes and smoke it, it makes them feel happy.'

'Why can't they smoke it if they want to?' I explained that the government knew it was bad for people's health and it cost a lot of money to make them well again. So people are not allowed to grow it and are punished if they do.

Sophie said, 'When the police take it away perhaps they smoke it.'

'Oh no' I said, 'They are the police, they wouldn't do anything like that.'

In the days that followed, boredom soon returned. I tried listening to the radio while pedalling but the sound quality was poor and I couldn't find any programmes I liked.

Then I devised a points system to provide some interest.

The highest score, five points, is for sighting a pedestrian with a dog, a disabled mobility scooter is four points, a taxi three points, a bicycle two points and, at the bottom of the scale, a bus one point. To save complications nothing else merits any points. To date, my highest score is twenty-seven.

Yesterday morning, after five minutes of strenuous pedalling, I spotted five points coming down the road - a heavily built, middle-aged man with a black dog on a lead. As I watched the dog stopped, squatted down and, while its master waited patiently, deposited a big, sausage like poo in the middle of the pavement.

I wondered whether, as the street was empty of pedestrians, the man might take the easy option, ignore it and walk away. I was impressed when, taking something made of thin, transparent plastic from his pocket, he bent down and picked up the dog mess.

'What a splendid chap' I thought, 'a model citizen.'

He walked a few yards further down the street and, as he passed a neat, well-tended garden, leaned over the fence and tossed the package onto the immaculate lawn.

He walked on without a backward glance.

I changed my opinion of him as a model citizen and deducted five points from that day's score.

I Hate Cuckoos

Cuckoo! Cuckoo! this bird is a pest
Laying its egg in a little bird's nest
Cuckoo! Cuckoo! such a boring note
Sounds like the song has got stuck in its throat.

When it's grown enough and ready to fly
It's off to Africa without a good-bye
It's a murderous, greedy, ungrateful bird
Thank goodness by August it's no longer heard.

If I had a gun and was a reasonable shot
That cuckoo would soon end up in the pot
We could try cuckoo pie: eat something new
Or if you preferred, we could have cuckoo stew.

Disappointment

When reading her poems
I see *come hither* eyes
She's tall, dark and sexy
And has ravishing thighs.

When seen in the flesh
It's really too bad
She's plump, fat and forty
And looks slightly mad.

Her voice is too loud
And her hair is too thin
Her bottom sticks out
And she's blotchy of skin.

I'm sorry I've met her,
Love poems were nice
But now that I've seen her
They no longer entice.

Old Age

Now he's eighty and painfully thin,
Nothing left except bones and skin
What hair is left, more white than grey
He's had another lonely day.

He's fallen twice, the concrete's hard,
Once in the cellar and once in the yard.
Doesn't seem long since he was in his prime
It's hard to believe the passage of time.

He's tired of all the pills and potions
And trying crazy way-out notions.
Then there's the hearing and the sight
And waking often in the night.

A replaced hip and a rebuilt knee
Can't go long without having a pee.
Aching legs and painful feet
It's hard to walk across the street.

His shoulders droop, his back is bent
He knows his time is nearly spent.
The future looks alarmingly dire
To be laid in a coffin and into the fire.

Meeting the Vicar

As I went down St George's street
I heard the vicar say
'Lovely to meet you Miss Murgatroyd
On such a sunny day.'

He enquired about my age
I said I'm eighty-four
He said 'Dear lady when you pop off
I'll see you through heaven's door.'

I could tell that he'd been drinking,
I could smell communion wine
So I hit him with my walking stick
And said 'You drunken swine!'

Matches

With the addition
Of friction
I will burst into flame
I can pass it to others
A dangerous game

If you are willing
To part with a shilling
You can buy about fifty
Which has got to be thrifty

If you have plenty of matches
And are working to scale
You can build bridges and castles
Your efforts won't fail

If you look in the box
And take out just five
They'll make you a Lowry
But he'll never survive

He lit a fag
Threw the match in the bin
And left the room
A stupid sin.

The house went up
There was nothing left
His wife came home
She was quite bereft

She said to a fireman
'Have you seen Mr Trinder?'
'That's him over there…
That big black cinder.'

English

'What's that mark in the piece of wood, Dad?'
'It's called a knot.'
'A not?'
'It's not a not, it's a knot.'
'That's what I said, dad.'
'You spelt it wrong.'
'I didn't spell it dad.'
'But you would if you did.'
'How do you know, dad?'
'Spell it then.'
'N O T'
'There you are, it's spelt K N O T.'
'I didn't hear you say k-not, dad.'
'You don't sound the 'K' son.'
'Why have it then? Sounds stupid to me, dad.'
'There are lots more son…
Knack, knapsack, kneel, knob, knock,
knee, know, knobble, knickers…'
'Dad!'
'There's 'G's as well…
Gnat, gnash, gnaw, gnome, all silent.'
'Sounds daft to me dad.'
'English is a beautiful language, son.'
'If you say so dad, not very easy is it?'

The Reverend Lewis's Camera

It was his forty-fifth birthday; the Rev Jeremy Lewis was sitting at the kitchen table opening his birthday cards, his wife watching.

There were not many, the one from his parents contained a Marks and Spencer gift voucher.

There was only one present (from his wife) he carefully unwrapped it revealing a brightly coloured box with a picture of a camera on it.

He took the camera out; it was small, shiny silver and felt surprisingly solid. On the front, next to the lens was the one word 'ADVENT'

'It's digital' said his wife 'and I thought the make was suitable for your profession.

You don't have to buy any film for it, the man in the shop said if you just take the card in they will make prints for you... and it doesn't cost very much to have them made.'

'Thank you, my dear, I shall enjoy it. After breakfast I'll sit down and read the instruction book to see how it works.'

In the afternoon he told his wife he was going out to try the camera, 'I'll go down to the beach... take my swimming trunks, I might have a dip.'

He climbed down the steep path to the almost deserted, end of season, sandy beach, snapping pictures as he went.

Two sunbathing girls hidden behind some rocks watched him as he went to his favourite sheltered spot. They saw him remove his clerical grey trousers and underpants, lay them down on a rock and place his little camera on top of them. They saw him pull on his bathing trunks before taking off his shirt, which he then placed over the camera.

As soon as he had run down the beach and into the sea, the girls went quickly to where his clothes were neatly stacked. One of the girls took the camera from its hiding place while the other sat on the rock beside his clothes.

60

The photograph was quickly taken and the two girls, laughing, went back to their sunbathing.

A week later, his wife went grocery shopping. Before leaving she took the card out of Jeremy's camera the way the man in the shop had showed her. She went in and asked him for a set of prints, 'No just one set, thank you, yes glossy will be fine.'

She paid for the prints and on returning to her car decided to have a quick preview.

A lovely shot of the church in the evening sunlight, some pink sea thrift, some rock formations, jolly good camera she thought, lovely sharp photographs.

Then a picture of a pretty girl, smiling at the camera, her bikini top laying on the rock next to Jeremy's clothes and wearing his dog collar round her neck!

'Wait till I get home!'

She started the car and shot forward at a fast pace, unlike her usual careful driving.

When she was home she called to her husband who was at his desk writing next Sunday's sermon.

She pulled up a chair and sat beside him, 'Surprise, I've got your photographs for you.'

'Thank you dear.' he said.

As he went to take them out of the packet, she gave him a frosty glare.

'What's the matter... aren't they any good?'

'They're very good, very sharp, very clear and plenty of detail... and you've got some serious explaining to do.' she said.

Breakfast

It happens every morning
It's always the same
I see you at the breakfast table
And I fall in love again.

Writing Poems

Since starting to write poems
Something's happened to me
And I'm afraid it's getting worse
Everything I think, everything I say
Keeps turning into verse.

The doctor said
You must stay in bed
I'm afraid there is no cure
Don't give up hope, learn how to cope
It's verbal diarrhoea.

Newport Girl

There was a young lady from Newport
Whose business was import and export
She earned most of her cash
By having a bash
In the back of her supercharged Escort.

The Fair

He sat thinking of a day, when he was twelve years old.

He had always hated his name, Oliver, sometimes shortened to Ollie, which he hated even more.

His Mum and Dad were divorced. He lived with his Mum in a cottage on the outskirts of a small, mainly Georgian coastal town in Suffolk.

He often sat in his bedroom gazing out of the window. In the field opposite, the farmer grew wheat, at certain times of the year there was much interesting activity for him to watch. Beyond the field, in the grounds of the big house... the ancestral home of Squire Loftus... was a noisy rookery. Beyond this again lay the town with the tall white lighthouse in one of the streets and then the sea.

That year as always, the June bank holiday fair had come to Gun Hill.

Sitting in his bedroom with the window open, intermingled with the cries of rooks he could hear the enticing music of a fairground organ.

He longed to be there. He went downstairs, found his Mum and said, 'Can we go to the fair Mum?'

'No Oliver, I hate fairs! Noisy and vulgar.'

'Please Mum.'

She opened her purse and gave him a handful of coins, 'Here you are, you can spend it all, you needn't bring any back, enjoy yourself... and don't be late.'

'Thanks Mum.'

He walked the mile and a half to the fairground. In the fading daylight Gun Hill was like fairyland.

He went on the steam horses – twice, the chairaplane, the helter-skelter, the dodgems and the shooting range. He rolled coins, although he tried three times they never landed on a prize winning square. He had just enough money left to buy a stick of rock, not the pink peppermint kind but stripy brown

63

with a crunchy texture and delicious flavour. He remembered it well but never rediscovered it.

As he ate he wandered over to the line of ancient cannons pointing out to sea. He leant on one, sucking the last remnant of his rock.

He thought of an often told local story.

It was said soldiers had come to Gun Hill to fire a salute in honour of Queen Victoria 's marriage to Prince Albert . When the signal was given to fire, one of the guns failed to go off.

The soldier in charge walked round to the front of the cannon, as he foolishly looked into the barrel, the cannon went off, removing his head.

Oliver walked home, tired and happy, as he let himself into the cottage his Mum called,

'I thought I told you not to be late!'

'Sorry Mum.'

'Did you spend all the money?'

'All gone Mum.'

'Did you enjoy yourself?'

'Smashing!'

'That's good; you'd better get straight to bed now. Good night Oliver.'

'Night Mum and thanks.'

Advice for Poets No.2

If you want to write a poem
Make sure it doesn't rhyme
To write like Wendy Cope
Has now become a crime.

Staying Alive

The money's all gone but I have the state pension
There's a problem with health that I'd rather not mention.
I have three pairs of glasses it's a bit of a fiddle
One pair is for distance, one close and one middle.

I have plenty of teeth so I don't look a fright
But some are too loose and some are too tight.
There's an electronic gadget stuck in my ear
It whistles and twitters, but it helps me to hear.

In the medicine drawer are ten kinds of pills
One of each daily helps combat the ills
Attached to my heart something clever keeps pace
If it wasn't for this, I'd be out of the race.

Our wonderful medics don't want us to die
The more likely it is, the harder they try.
When we've had quite enough and we'd like to depart
It's illegal to help us, so they may not take part.

Don't think this is sad, 'cause I think it's funny
If the outlook is black, I imagine it's sunny.
I have plenty of food to fill up the belly
And in the evening, there's always the telly!

Sunday Lunch

Uncle Bill and Aunty Mary
Were eating lunch of roast canary
Uncle Bill said 'the outlook's bleak
I've only got the legs and beak'
Aunty Mary raised her voice
'I did the cooking, I have first choice'
'Next time' he said 'get something big
Like a ginger cat or a black spot pig.'

Newport City

Cerys Rhys-Davis and her husband Tom
Were struggling along the Brighton prom.
Blowing a gale and shockingly wet
As holidays go it's the worst one yet.

Cerys exclaimed 'I've had more than enough
Take me home now or I'll get in a huff.'
In the whole of their lives they've never been wetter.
They drove home to Wales and were soon feeling better.

'You can stuff bloody Brighton.' said Tom being coarse
'But to go there again I'd need dragging by force.'
'I don't like your language but I fully agree
I just want to stay well away from the sea.'

Newport has blue skies and Newport is sunny
Compared to Brighton it's all milk and honey
Newport we love, Newport 's stupendous
The people of Newport are simply tremendous.

Mrs Scarrott's Parrot

My very good friend Sebastian Scarrott
Bought his wife a big grey parrot.
It swore loudly all day and whistled all night
Mrs Scarrot decided she'd give it a fright.

That very night she woke in a strop
'That noisy damn bird is heading for the chop.'
She went downstairs and found a hatchet
Took the bird outside, ready to dispatch it.

The parrot said 'Missus spare me please.'
He looked appealing down on his knees.
She opened the cage, the bird took fright
Pecked her goodbye and flew into the night.

Bee Sting

We lay side by side
In the long green grass
The sun beat down
I was stung on the arse.

I complained to Julie
This is rather a farce
I was going to kiss you
But I'm stung on the arse.

Julie just giggled
Well it's come to a pass
If you're not going to kiss me
Because you're stung on the arse.

Lets take a photo
Have it framed under glass
Then everyone can see
The sting on your arse.

Harry and the Pistols

Patrick spotted Harry's huge American estate car as it nosed its way through the gateway and into the drive. He was down the steps from the front door before the car had stopped moving. Disappointed to see the car was empty.

'I hoped you'd have some choice, irresistible antique that would tempt currency notes to fly out of the safe in your direction.'

'I could sell you this splendid car.'

'No chance! I wouldn't be seen dead in it Harry. Mind you, painted black it would be good for coffins. I thought you loved it.

'I do! But now, after a few weeks with it I've found some drawbacks. It's too conspicuous; I keep being told where I've been seen. Twelve miles to the gallon's a bit salty and except on motorways or dual carriageways it's tricky to overtake. I love it but it'll have to go; I think I'll go back to a Volvo. I've brought you something to make your eyes light up; it's on the front seat.'

He opened the car door and removed a flat mahogany box.

'Can it be what I hope it is Harry?'

'Yep, a cased pair of pistols and all the accessories.'

'Flintlock?'

'A bit later, percussion cap, but mint condition.'

'Come into the kitchen Harry, Ursula's coffee and Swiss biscuits will ease the passage of a deal.'

Ursula poured coffee and said 'Those I should so much like to shoot fire with… a licence shall we perhaps need?'

'No licence, not for muzzle-loaders, but it's against the law to shoot anyone with them.'

'Sometimes naughty Patrick I would like to shoot!'

A buzzer sounded announcing the entry of customers.

'Ursula said 'With this I shall cope, try if you can to let our much loved Patrick to have a bargain, there's a good boy

Harry.'

'I always give him bargains! I can't imagine how much he's made out of me since our first deal… but no hard feelings.'

They completed the deal, Harry pocketed the money and left.

Patrick wrote a price ticket in a code only he and Ursula understood; even Harry had been unable to crack it. He took the box into the showroom and placed it on a leather topped pedestal desk. He opened the box and took out one of the pistols which he laid temptingly in front of the box.

A percussion-cap pistol requires a copper cap containing a charge of gunpowder to be fitted over the nipple. When the trigger is pulled the hammer smacks down on the cap sending a flame into the barrel setting off the main charge. The nipple can be damaged by pulling the trigger with no cap in place.

Prospective customers seemed unable to resist cocking the gun and pulling the trigger without a cap in place. Patrick, became annoyed, fitted a percussion cap and cocked the pistol. The next person to pull the trigger would be surprised by a loud report. Strangely none of the customers during the next few days touched the pistol and Patrick forgot about setting his booby trap.

Some antique dealing friends called in, Mr Clingan, a retired bank manager and his wife. To provide interest in his retirement they'd bought a small shop with a pretty bow window in a nearby village. They took up antique dealing and were enjoying their new life-style. They liked dainty porcelain and small, useful, pieces of furniture rather than real collectors' items.

They wandered happily round the showroom and before Patrick could do anything to stop him, Mr Clingan picked up the pistol, pointed it at his wife and pulled the trigger. There was a loud bang and a cloud of smoke. Mr Clingan, as white as a sheet, staggered back and slumped into a chair.

Patrick rushed to the kitchen and returned with a glass of

70

water. Mr Clingan took one of his heart pills.

Patrick apologised profusely and said he hadn't realised it was such a stupid thing to do.

When Mr Clingan felt better he said' 'It was my own fault Patrick, everyone knows you should never point a gun at anyone, even if it's antique and not loaded.

They left with a pair of porcelain figures and a small Georgian hanging bookshelf.

Mr Clingan lived for several more years and remained a good customer.

Boy Racer

I'm not yet sixteen
Too young for a test
So I've stolen this car
It's one of the best

If I put down my foot
She'll do a hundred and twenty
When it comes to raw power
This baby's got plenty.

We really were speeding
When we shot round the bend
Smashed into a lamp-post
And that was the end.

The flowers were pretty
The gravestone is smart
I'm sorry this happened
It's broken mum's heart.

Bing Bang Bong

Bing, bang, bong
What a stinky pong
Ding, dong, dell
Such a nasty smell.

I s'pose you think it's smart
To release a secret fart.
And pretend it wasn't you
Phew, phew, phew.

Nig, nag, nog
Blame it on the dog
Blim, blam, blink
I can't believe the stink.

Sophie's lunch

A pretty little girl
Named Sophie Jones
Was eating fish,
It was full of bones.

She laid the bones
All round her plate
Said 'Bones in fish
I really hate!'

She liked the peas
And she liked the chips
But bony fish
Won't pass her lips.

Sausages she thinks,
Are really good
With potatoes, gravy
And Yorkshire pud.

Ice cream for afters
Is a tasty treat
With hot fudge sauce
It can't be beat.

Five Star Restaurant

Jim said 'Let's go for some luxury nosh
I know of a place, it's frightfully posh.'
I've already phoned and booked a table
I used to go with my wealthy aunt Mabel

Which fork to use? I felt out of place
I feared my manners might be a disgrace
Haughty waiters look down their noses
The effeminate toilets smelling of roses

The maitre D with his airs and graces
Making sure we know our places
Working chaps are not welcome here
They drink champagne, but we drink beer

It was never meant for the likes of us
We try to eat quietly without any fuss
It's true the food is the finest ever
Will we come here again? The answer's *never.*

Lion Hunter

Daniel Petersen went to Rhodesia to shoot lions. He took his new wife with him. This was in the days when shooting wildlife was carried out with a rifle rather than a camera.

Daniel's name was never shortened to Dan but his friends knew him as Pelican Petersen or Pelly for short. This was because, in his schooldays, he could stuff a huge quantity of food into his mouth in one go. He was not greedy; it was just that he had a good appetite and liked to get on with everything as quickly as possible.

His wife's maiden name was Navatarola Palonska. She was a ballet dancer before she married Pelican and moved with him to Africa . She travelled with him through the bush helping with the lions he shot, skinning, packing, making herself generally useful and organising shipping the skins back to England They were in great demand to be hung on castle walls or laid snarling on the floors of homes of the aristocracy. Lion skins sold for large sums of money and Pelly became wealthy.

When they had been in Africa for about two years Navatarola fell pregnant. After nine months her belly had grown to an impressive size and assisted by two fat Bantu women she gave birth on the fourteenth of May nineteen thirty two. The birth commenced at thirty minutes after midnight and finished at four in the morning. The first baby, a sturdy boy, was taken by the two Bantu women helpers, washed in water from the river and laid naked in soft dry grass on the hard earth floor of the shelter. The weather was hot, perfect for naked babies.

After thirty minutes respite Navatarola began to groan and shortly gave birth to a baby girl, smaller than the boy but crying lustily. Thirty more minutes and another girl was born and just before four o clock in the morning baby number four arrived, another boy. These three joined the first boy and they all lay in a neat row in the soft dry grass.

Pelly returned from the hunting and strode into the clearing followed by his Bantu team of hunters and a large shot male lion, its legs tied to a pole and carried by four of his strongest men.

He went into the shelter, kissed his exhausted wife and went to view the new arrivals. He was overwhelmed; he went back and kissed Navatarola again, told her she'd done a grand job and went out to tell the hunters the news. He sat with them round the camp fire until dawn was breaking and then climbed into his hammock.

Navatarola and the two fat Bantu women fed the babies and gave them much love, but they failed to flourish. After a few weeks only the first born, the biggest, strongest and hungriest of the four survived. Pelly said they should call him Leo to remind them of the lions he'd shot; the lions that had been so good for the bank balance. Navatarola wanted to call him Alexander… 'Because he's great,' she said.

She took several weeks to recover her strength, during this time Pelly shot several more lions and felt he'd pretty well cleared the area.

Navatarola was tired and fed up with the life they were leading. 'This too hot country is not a nice place to grow up Pelly and is not good for me as well… I want to go home and if you won't come I shall on my own go and Leo Alexander shall come with me.'

'Darling' said Pelly , 'You look gorgeous when you're cross. If you want to leave Africa I'm coming with you. There must be something I can shoot in England .'

They made the long journey to the coast where they boarded a tramp steamer with their luggage and many crates of valuable commodities acquired on the hunting expedition.

The tramp steamer was small, the sea rough, gale force winds howled and the rain came in non stop torrents. Navatarola spent most of the voyage in her berth longing for stillness. Leo Alexander cried.

Pelly spent the daylight hours on deck in his waterproofs and most of the hours of darkness in the Captain's cabin where they exchanged hardly believable stories of events in their past lives and drank Scotch whisky.

They docked at Tilbury; Carter Paterson sent one of their lorries to pick up Pelly's crates and most of the luggage. They transported it all to one of their depositories where it would be safe until needed.

Pelly and his small family took a taxi to Paddington and boarded a train (First class) for the long, tedious journey to Truro . They planned to stay here with his aged parents while he hunted for a new home. He disliked his parents intensely, particularly his father but he said to Navatarola 'It won't be for long Nav, it's a case of any old port in a storm.'

He had no idea where they would settle. 'Just as long as it's miles away from Truro , Nav.'

'You're an ungrateful Englishman, Pel, don't you think?'

'Indeed I do… always have been, too late to change now darling.'

His property hunting eventually took him to Norfolk ; he liked Norfolk and found a substantial house with a satisfactorily small garden. He had the house decorated and electricity installed. He furnished a bedroom and the kitchen, deciding to leave everything else until his wife arrived.

He sent for Navatarola and Leo Alexander. He knew he ought to go down and collect them but couldn't face another encounter with his father. So he left Navatarola to manage the train journey with little Leo on her own. He drove to Norwich station in his new Lagonda coupé and met them off the train. Navatarola was tired and snappy, he kissed her but the response was not warm. Leo was bawling. 'Hungry' she said.

He picked up her case, took Leo in his other arm and led them to the car.

'That is not yours, I hope?'

'I bought it last week… beautiful isn't it' he said proudly.

78

'Horrible!' she said, 'Big, flashy, vulgar and green cars I hate!'

Pelly was silent, He loaded the case into the boot and when they placed Leo on the back seat he gurgled with pleasure.

'He thinks it's OK.'

'Not old enough to have any sense!'

'I thought you'd be sure to like it, Nav.'

'Well, wrong is what you thought then, didn't you.'

She was still tired and snappy. 'A better job of choosing a house I hope you've made.'

Pelly heaved a sigh, suddenly he felt uncertain.

They left the railway station and Pelly drove steadily for three quarters of an hour to 'Redehall Villa' their new home, both his passengers were asleep. He jumped out, leaving his door open to avoid the noise of slamming, ran to the house, unlocked the door, switched on lights and returned to the Lagonda for his family. Navatarola was awake, Leo still sleeping. She said, 'Sorry Pelly for recent remarks, the car I like after all, smooth, quiet and comfy, but the green colour, still I hate.' Pelly snorted 'Not green… *British Racing Green.*'

Carrying her case he gave her a quick tour of the house, leaving her case in the bedroom as they went round. They went into the kitchen 'This house I like,' she said as she poured milk for Leo into a brand new shiny saucepan and put it on the stove to heat. 'This so modern electric cooker I like also, you have well done Pelly .'

She went out to the car and woke Leo, he opened his mouth wide to howl and she stuck the bottle straight into the opening. He changed his mind about howling and began to suck furiously. She changed him on the kitchen table, carried him up to the nursery, tucked him into his cot and he went straight to sleep. Pelly watched all this with fascination, Navatarola turned to him, 'Such a good boy my little Alexander is.' He slept until eight-thirty the next morning.

They spent the next few days in the Norwich furniture shops

and in a couple of weeks their house had become a comfortable home.

Pelly sat in the punt, six o clock in the morning and chilly. He had his rifle across his knees and waited   He heard a regular squeaking sound and raised his gun. The sound caused by strong wings beating through the early morning air. Out of the mist the swan appeared flying low and fast. From force of habit he took careful, calculated aim. He had no intention of shooting – *swans - property of the crown – not on any account to be killed.*

He kept the bird in his sites and when it was exactly level with him, pulled the trigger. The swan, no longer animated, heavy as a stone, plummeted into the still water.

Pel was stunned, not by his marksmanship but by the fact he had actually shot a swan. He unhitched the punt and paddled to where the swan floated in a spreading red stain. He hauled it into the punt, stuffed it into a sack and wondered if they were good to eat. He decided he'd better not let Nav see it and stayed on until he'd shot a goose. The goose was standing on the ground feeding, an easy shot...

He put it into another sack, put the sacks into the boot of his Lagonda and drove home.

He collected a spade from the tool shed and carried the sack containing the swan to the bottom of the garden. He dug a deep hole of sufficient size, took the swan out of the sack and dropped it into the hole, at this moment Navatarola came down the garden calling, 'In fifteen minutes is time for breakfast.' She was curious to find out what Pelly was up to, walked up to him and looked in the hole' 'This I do not believe Pel. A swan you shoot dead!' she said accusingly.

'It was an accident, Nav.'

'Such a good shot I see, straight through the eye. An accident, I think not!'

80

'I didn't mean to pull the trigger, it just happened.'

'This grave you must quickly fill, Pell, nothing will we say.'

She shrugged her shoulders and went back into the house.

Pell shovelled earth, tramped over the mound to make it as flat as possible, returned the spade to the shed and went in for breakfast.

They had been in Norfolk for two years. One evening Pelly said, 'I'm sick and tired of eating goose, duck and rabbit; I want to shoot something bigger, Nav.'

'The goose is fast and big, for you a good target Pel.'

'I'm tired of shooting geese, I want to shoot stags. How would you like to move to Scotland , Nav?'

'Here I love, Scotland is no! Darker, colder, far away and I hear of biting midges. If you go to Scotland , I stay here.'

'What about a holiday Nav? Three months maybe.'

'For you, yes… Alexander and me we can be happy to stay here.'

Pel began to make plans to go to Scotland on his own, but on September the third nineteen thirty-nine World War II started. Pelly joined the army and became a sniper. He shot men and found this more rewarding than shooting geese, better even than shooting lions.

On the 14th of April 1942 he made a mistake and raised his head above the parapet, he was immediately shot in the neck; the bullet went in one side and out the other. There was no chance of survival, death almost immediate, he just had time to think 'So this is what it's like to be shot,' and he was dead.